MY UNCLE'S Dunkirk

Mick Manning and Brita Granström

W
FRANKLIN WATTS
LONDON • SYDNEY

IN ASSOCIATION
WITH

IMPERIAL WAR
MUSEUM

When I was a boy in the late 1960s, we'd go on holiday to my aunty and uncle's house by the sea. In the room where I slept, I found a box of magazines all about the Second World War. My dad told me my uncle had been a soldier in the war - at Dunkirk - but my uncle never spoke about it. I read the magazines at bedtime and that's how I found out about Dunkirk.

My uncle was a telephone engineer and drove a green van with a ladder on the roof. He spent his working day up telegraph poles or fixing junction boxes in leafy suburbs. He could be called out any time, day or night.

In 1940, he'd been a telephone engineer in the Royal Artillery. But there weren't any leafy suburbs on the front line – just cables stretching from command posts to artillery positions; worming through hedgerows criss-crossed by enemy gunfire, day and night.

But he never spoke about it . . .

In the Second World War, the artillery and other front-line army units kept in touch with their command posts by telephone. Laying the cables and keeping them connected was essential – and dangerous – work.

My uncle's car was a
Hillman Minx with
a cream stripe. It had
a furry little monkey
hanging on elastic from
the mirror. Sometimes we'd
tease him that he was a
slow driver and he'd smile to
himself and shake his head, as
if he knew something we didn't.

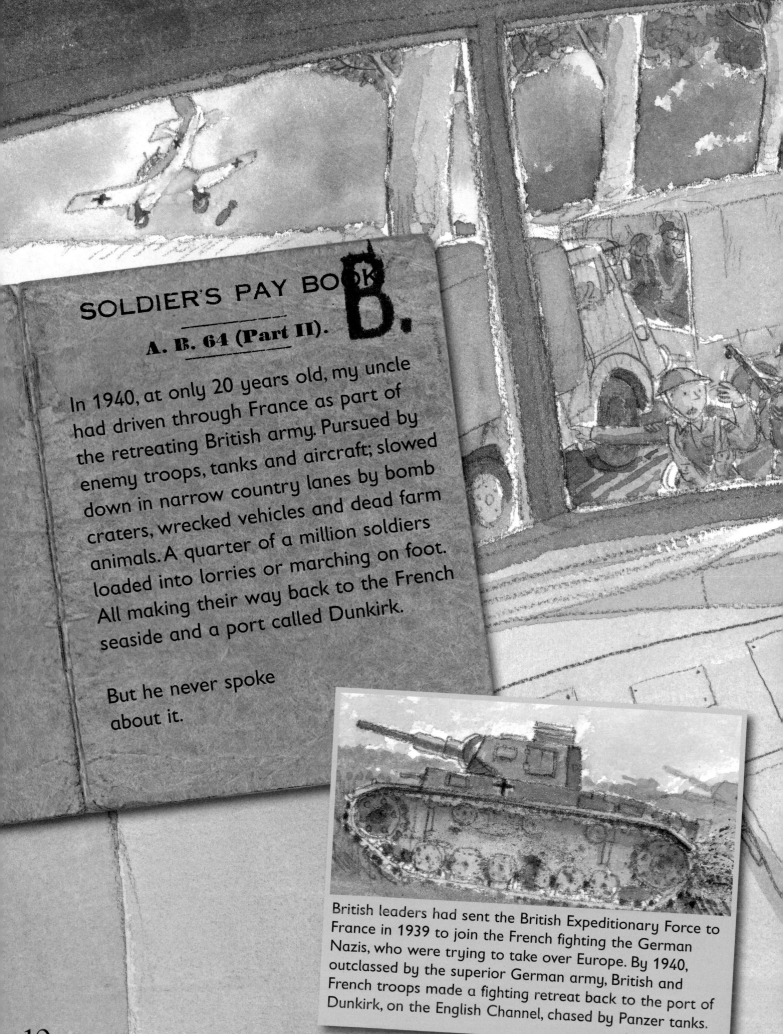

SOLDIER'S PAY BOOK

A. B. 64 (Part II). B.

In 1940, at only 20 years old, my uncle had driven through France as part of the retreating British army. Pursued by enemy troops, tanks and aircraft; slowed down in narrow country lanes by bomb craters, wrecked vehicles and dead farm animals. A quarter of a million soldiers loaded into lorries or marching on foot. All making their way back to the French seaside and a port called Dunkirk.

But he never spoke about it.

British leaders had sent the British Expeditionary Force to France in 1939 to join the French fighting the German Nazis, who were trying to take over Europe. By 1940, outclassed by the superior German army, British and French troops made a fighting retreat back to the port of Dunkirk, on the English Channel, chased by Panzer tanks.

Almost half a million British and French soldiers were trapped with their backs to the sea. The only hope was a rescue operation. But how could half a million soldiers be rescued in only a few days?

When my mum and dad took me for summer holidays, it was brilliant. My aunty would make picnics, my uncle bought ice-creams and we'd spend all day on the beach. I'd dig in the sand, watch the seagulls and listen to the peaceful sound of the sea.

There were tens of thousands of troops; enough men to fill three major football stadiums, all hoping for rescue and under regular attack from the air by Stuka dive bombers.

Here's another one, Doc...

In 1940, when my uncle arrived at Dunkirk, he spent all day on the beach, and the next day, and the day after that. He had dug in the sand, but not for fun. He couldn't hear the sea for the sound of gunfire and the seagulls had all flown away.

But he never spoke about it . . .

16

On the seafront I saw holidaymakers of
all shapes and sizes paddling in the sea.
And there were queues everywhere:
queues for the pier, queues for the
cinema, queues for ice-cream.

My uncle hated queues . . .
and he never went paddling.

He'd queued with his mates and other soldiers;
thousands of them, strung out in long lines.
Some queued for large ships in the harbour
while others gathered on the beaches to meet
the smaller boats that could get into the bay.

As they waded out to meet the boats, up to their waists in the waves, the sea chilled them to the bone and they were shelled, machine-gunned and bombed. But the survivors had still queued up to be rescued. They had still queued up!

For free repetition of doubtful words telep~~ ~~ at office of delivery. Other enquiries shoul~~ ~~ TELEGRAMS ENQUIRY " or ~~ ~~ mpanied by this form and, if pos~~ ~~ 20 13 ~~ ~~

The British mounted a huge rescue operation called Operation Dynamo. Under almost constant enemy fire, soldiers boarded British destroyers and other large ships from the harbour while others had to wade toward the ships from the beach. But more boats were still needed.

Move along lads...

We've been here for hours!

Sometimes we'd go and watch holidaymakers boarding the pleasure steamer. Puffs of smoke came from the funnel and people would wave at us from the deckchairs and railings.

21

The Navy couldn't get enough people off the beaches in time with the ships it had, so steamers, fishing boats and even tiny boats like the 15-foot-long *Tamzine* took their chance. They could get closer to the beach than the big ships and although many were destroyed, the 'little ships' saved thousands of soldiers.

We're full!

POST OFFICE STAMP SHOWING DATE OF PAYMENT

War Gratuity and Post War Credits deposited
in Post Office Savings Bank..............

There were puffs of smoke
and people waving at
Dunkirk, that's for sure;
waving and screaming as
crowded ships got dive-
bombed. Weary troops who
thought they'd been saved
suddenly found their rescue
ships exploding and sinking.
The survivors struggled
ashore only to rejoin the
dreadful queues.

But my uncle never
spoke about it.

23

I liked beachcombing. I'd find shells, seaweed, old deckchairs, dead crabs, dead jellyfish; the sea always washes dead things onto the beach . . .

Look what I've found!

My uncle didn't like beachcombing . . .

28

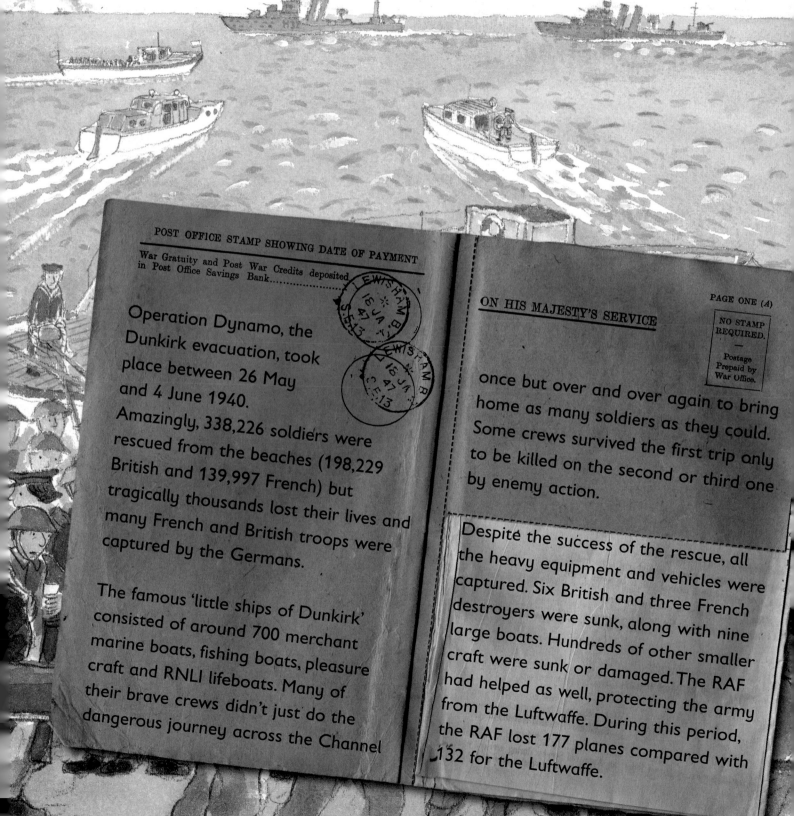

My uncle was one of the lucky ones. He got back to England safely on one of the ships. But he never spoke about Dunkirk or what he saw ... or the mates he'd left behind. He never spoke about it to anyone.

POST OFFICE STAMP SHOWING DATE OF PAYMENT

War Gratuity and Post War Credits deposited in Post Office Savings Bank.......................

Operation Dynamo, the Dunkirk evacuation, took place between 26 May and 4 June 1940. Amazingly, 338,226 soldiers were rescued from the beaches (198,229 British and 139,997 French) but tragically thousands lost their lives and many French and British troops were captured by the Germans.

The famous 'little ships of Dunkirk' consisted of around 700 merchant marine boats, fishing boats, pleasure craft and RNLI lifeboats. Many of their brave crews didn't just do the dangerous journey across the Channel

ON HIS MAJESTY'S SERVICE

PAGE ONE (4)

NO STAMP REQUIRED.
—
Postage Prepaid by War Office.

once but over and over again to bring home as many soldiers as they could. Some crews survived the first trip only to be killed on the second or third one by enemy action.

Despite the success of the rescue, all the heavy equipment and vehicles were captured. Six British and three French destroyers were sunk, along with nine large boats. Hundreds of other smaller craft were sunk or damaged. The RAF had helped as well, protecting the army from the Luftwaffe. During this period, the RAF lost 177 planes compared with 132 for the Luftwaffe.

My uncle's souvenirs

When my uncle died in 1991, my aunty gave me a plastic bag she'd found in his tool shed. In it were some souvenirs from his old army days. Looking at the things he'd saved made me want to write this book and I have included them so you can see for yourself.

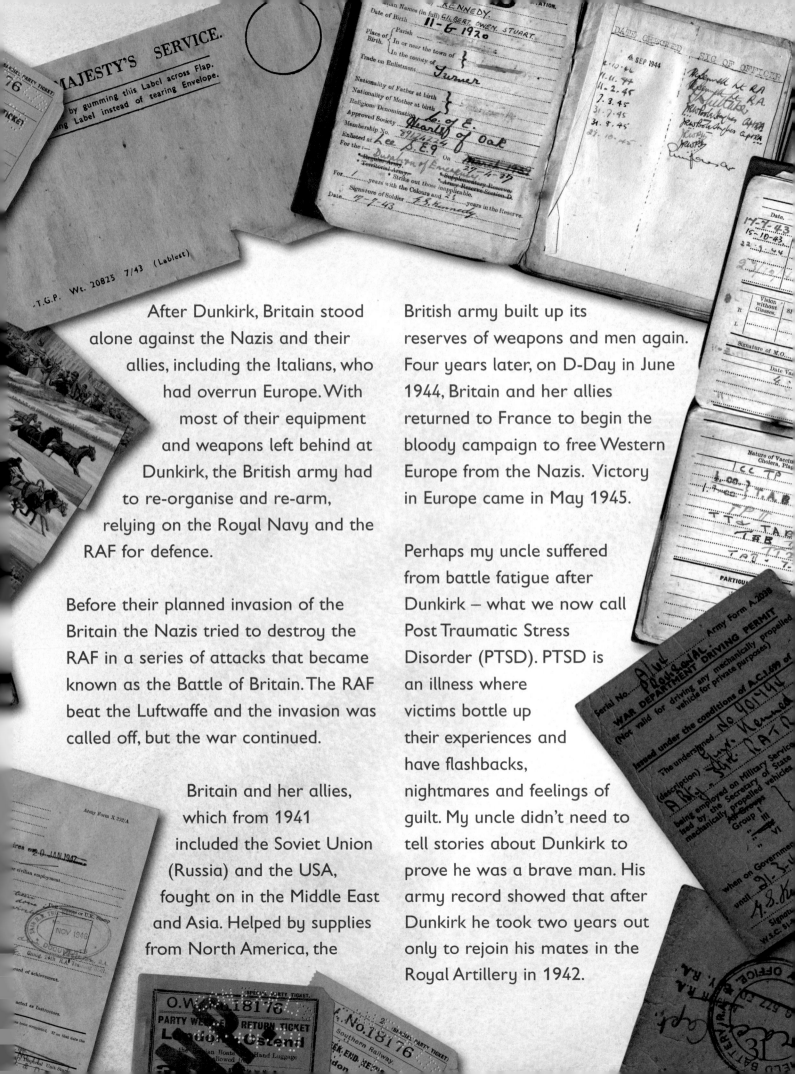

After Dunkirk, Britain stood alone against the Nazis and their allies, including the Italians, who had overrun Europe. With most of their equipment and weapons left behind at Dunkirk, the British army had to re-organise and re-arm, relying on the Royal Navy and the RAF for defence.

Before their planned invasion of the Britain the Nazis tried to destroy the RAF in a series of attacks that became known as the Battle of Britain. The RAF beat the Luftwaffe and the invasion was called off, but the war continued.

Britain and her allies, which from 1941 included the Soviet Union (Russia) and the USA, fought on in the Middle East and Asia. Helped by supplies from North America, the British army built up its reserves of weapons and men again. Four years later, on D-Day in June 1944, Britain and her allies returned to France to begin the bloody campaign to free Western Europe from the Nazis. Victory in Europe came in May 1945.

Perhaps my uncle suffered from battle fatigue after Dunkirk – what we now call Post Traumatic Stress Disorder (PTSD). PTSD is an illness where victims bottle up their experiences and have flashbacks, nightmares and feelings of guilt. My uncle didn't need to tell stories about Dunkirk to prove he was a brave man. His army record showed that after Dunkirk he took two years out only to rejoin his mates in the Royal Artillery in 1942.

More information and explanations

allies: In war, countries or groups that fight together.

British Expeditionary Force: The name given to the land forces sent by the British to fight in mainland Europe in 1939 and 1940 at the start of the Second World War.

destroyer: a fast warship used for escorting convoys and attacking submarines.

engineer: in the army, a soldier who specialises in building bridges and fortifications and setting up communication links.

front line: in a battle, the position nearest to the enemy where fighting takes place.

'Little ships of Dunkirk': the collection of non-military ships and boats, many crewed by civilian volunteers, that helped in Operation Dynamo.

Luftwaffe: the German air force.

Nazis: the National Socialists (Nazi), the political party led by Adolf Hitler that ruled Germany from 1933 to the end of the Second World War.

Operation Dynamo: the name given to the rescue operation mounted between 26 May and 4 June 1940 to collect British and French troops stranded at Dunkirk.

Panzer: a German tank, an armoured vehicle used in combat.

RAF: the Royal Air Force, Britain's air force.

RNLI: the Royal National Life Boat Institution, Britain's volunteer sea rescue service.

Royal Artillery: the part of the British army that specialise in operating guns, such as cannons and rocket launchers.

Royal Navy: Britain's sea force.

Second World War: a war fought in Europe, Africa and Asia from 1939 to 1945. An alliance of countries led by Britain, the Soviet Union (Russia) and the USA defeated another alliance including Germany, Italy and Japan.

Stuka dive bombers: German aircraft that dropped bombs with pinpoint accuracy. When they dived, sirens on the wheels made a terrifying noise.

You can find out much more about the Second World War by visiting the various Imperial War Museum (IWM) branches. You can even see one of the 'Little ships of Dunkirk', Tamzine (see page 26), at the IWM London. The IWM website lists their branches and gives lots more information: www.iwm.org.uk

This book is dedicated to my Uncle Gil (1920-1991)

This edition published in 2011 by Franklin Watts, 338 Euston Road, London, NW1 3BH

Franklin Watts Australia
Level 17/207 Kent Road, Sydney, NSW 2000

Text and illustrations © 2010
Mick Manning and Brita Granström

Mick and Brita made the illustrations for this book
Find out more about Mick and Brita on
www.mickandbrita.com

Editor: Rachel Cooke
Art director: Jonathan Hair

With many thanks to Terry Charman of the Imperial War Museum

Printed in China
A CIP catalogue record is available from the British Library.

Dewey Classification: 823.9'14

ISBN: 978 0 7496 9342 8

Franklin Watts is a division of Hachette Children's Books, an Hachette UK company.
www.hachette.co.uk